WHEN PRAYER
SEEMS TO FAIL

Michael Canion

Dedication

This book is dedicated to my wife and my mother. My mother has gone to be with the Lord, but her legacy of prayer and service live on in the many people she touched.

Table of Contents

Introduction

This book is a compilation of personal insights concerning prayer, articles and quotes by men and women of prayer. It is my hope that it will serve as a tool to help the reader develop a more intimate fellowship with God through prayer. It is a very personal book that chronicles some of the highs and lows of my walk with God. It is easy to share your successes, but somewhat unnerving to share your failures. There are things in the book that I hesitated to write, but in the final analysis, I felt compelled to write it. May God bless you and may the book be a blessing to you.

1

"Twenty Minutes"

Matthew 6:6 – "But when you pray, go into your room, close the door and pray to your Father, who is unseen. Then your Father, who sees what is done in secret, will reward you."

Portions of this chapter should really be my introduction. But, there are those of you, myself included, who habitually disregard the introduction and go directly to the first chapter. I felt as though this part was such an important part because it helps you understand my background.

For as long as I can remember, church has been a part of my life. My parents were active members of the Jones Avenue Church of God in Christ. Most Pentecostals are familiar with the Church of God in Christ and its founder, Bishop Charles Harrison Mason. Growing up in the Church of God in Christ, I heard many stories about Bishop Mason that were legendary concerning how God healed people through him, and he was widely known as being, first and foremost, a man of prayer.

Prayer was central in his life and the denomination. I remember one group in particular from the Church of God in

Christ called the Prayer and Bible Band. This was a group of women who went from house to house every week to meet, read scripture and pray. On occasion, they would come to our house and I would make a point not to be there. From my perspective, this was embarrassing because none of the kids wanted to come by my house and play because all of the praying going on. They prayed long and loud. I remember wishing they would just hold it down a bit, then maybe no one who hear them. They were rebuking the devil, talking about the blood of Jesus and talking in languages nobody understood.

I didn't realize that one day I would greatly appreciate every prayer that was prayed in that house. Without realizing it, prayer played a huge part in my life then and it does now.

However, one of my greatest impressions concerning prayer came from my father. There were days when after work, he would go to his room kneel and pray. Through the cracked door, I saw my father pray and my entire life, the mental picture of him praying has been seared into my mind. I did not understand prayer or why he was doing it, but there was a realization on my part that this was special, and because my father was doing it, that made it even more special. I would stand there motionless, silently peering through the cracked door, watching him on his knees as he said words that were barely audible, talking to someone I could not see. He could have been praying about any number of things and having a wife and seven children, I'm sure he had a great deal to pray about. My wife and I only have two and we stay pretty busy. My sister, Geraldine, in particular, was a piece of work. He may have spent more time praying for her and with good reason. She is saved and loves God dearly now, but back in the day, she loved to fight, stayed in trouble and didn't listen to anybody. In those days, if you saw her and a bear fighting, pray for the bear because he was soon to be a rug.

My father left me an example of prayer, even though I didn't realize it at the time. When I first received Christ, my goal was to be just like my father and Bishop Mason. Bishop Mason was known to pray for hours at a time and I wanted to be of the same mold. One day, not long after I had accepted Christ, I decided to go on a special consecration where I would fast and pray for three days.

I read the scripture where Jesus said, "When you pray, go into your closet, pray in secret and your Father, who is in secret, will reward you openly." With this in mind, off to the closet I went, ready to meet God, ready to pray for hours and be endued with power. Like Moses going to the mountain, I was prepared to meet God. In that closet, surrounded by coats and shirts as my prayer partners, I began to pray. I prayed for my family members, the nation, Africa, Asia, Europe and the Americas. I prayed for everybody and everything. It was hot in that closet and sweat was pouring off my face, but that was fine because to me, the sweat was indicative of my passionate, powerful praying.

When I ran out of people and things to pray for, silence filled the closet. There was a holy hush. Drenched in sweat, I slowly looked at my watch and realized that only twenty minutes had gone by.

Twenty minutes! Are you kidding me, twenty minutes, I thought.

I had prayed for the nations of the world, everyone in my family tree, the president, Democrats and Republicans and all it took was twenty minutes.

This began my matriculation into the school of prayer. It was on that day that I began this journey of learning to pray and learning that prayers are more than words.

"Prayer is a trade to be learned. We must be apprentices and serve our time at it. Painstaking care, much thought, practice and labour are required to be a skillful tradesman in praying. Practice in this, as well as in all other trades, makes perfect." – E.M.Bounds

The first mistake I made was to focus on the length of time I wanted to pray, which was the wrong goal. You cannot put your time with God on the clock because sometimes, you pray long and at other times, you don't. There were times when Jesus spent all night in prayer and they were times when He didn't.

I believe that great men and women of prayer prayed long hours for two reasons: one, they realized how deeply they needed God because they were faced with tremendous challenges and two, the more time they spent with Him, the more time they wanted to spend with Him. In other words, the quality of the fellowship grew. The goal was getting to know Him, learning how to relate to Him during the time they were together and allowing themselves to be changed by being in His presence. Peter prayed one of the shortest and most effective prayers recorded in the Bible. He said, "Lord save me" and in response to that prayer, he was saved. It is not necessarily the length of time that makes prayer effective, but there is certainly a place often neglected for unhurried extended time with God, however long or short the time may be.

"...True prayer is measured by weight, not by length. A single groan before God may have more fullness of prayer in it than a fine oration of great length." – C. H. Spurgeon

2

When Prayer Seems To Fail

"I look at the stonecutter hammering away at a rock a hundred times without so much as a crack showing in it, his efforts seem to no avail; yet at the 101st blow it splits in two. I know it was not the one blow that did it, but all that had gone before." – Jacob A Riis

*Luke 18:1-5 – Then Jesus told his disciples a parable to show them that they should **always pray** and not give up. [2] He said: "In a certain town there was a judge who neither feared God nor cared what people thought. [3] And there was a widow in that town who kept coming to him with the plea, 'Grant me justice against my adversary.' [4] "For some time he refused. But finally he said to himself, 'Even though I don't fear God or care what people think, [5] yet because this widow troubles me, I will see that she gets justice, lest by her continual coming she weary me!'"*

Stonecutting in the ancient world was a tedious exercise; it required time, patience, faith and work. Christians are called to be stonecutters, as well, because prayer is stonecutting of a different sort; it too requires time, patience, faith and work. Patience is non-negotiable when it comes to prayer because there are times we pray continually with no visible evidence that our praying is having any effect, but we must know that there are things happening that we cannot see. The stone of our circumstances may have the appearance of being unfazed, but if you could see inside the stone, you would notice a hairline crack in the middle, indicating that there is something happening that you cannot see. Since we cannot see it, we must believe that the collective strikes of our praying is weakening the stone of our circumstances.

One crucial prayer will work in conjunction with all those that have been prayed before and bring about change. Pray even though you are tired, pray when nothing seems to be changing, pray when you feel like it and pray when you don't. You and I must continue to strike with prayer because there is a blow that will bring deliverance, but only God knows which blow it is. Therefore, patience, perseverance and faith are necessary because we are ignorant as to when our change will come. Every day without fail, we must pray, even though it can be frustrating and discouraging to keep praying when nothing seems to change.

"It is hard to wait and press and pray, and hear no voice, but stay till the answer come." – E.M. Bounds

There are times when you strain to see something that will give you hope that change is near; anything will do, no matter how small. You look in vain for a cloud the size of a man's hand to give you hope that the rain will come, but there are no clouds in the sky and no hint that any will come. One of my favorite lines in a movie is from Morgan Freeman in the movie, "Deep Impact." He played the president and a young reporter thought she had him over a barrel. He said, "It may seem as though we have each other over a barrel, but I assure you it only seems that way." It may seem that your prayers are having no effect, but it only seems that way. Faith when praying is absolutely necessary because it is only by faith that you can keep striking when the stone seems to remain unfazed by neither the number of blows it has been struck nor the passion of the striker. However, you can wake up one day thinking it to be like the many that have gone before and as you raise your voice in prayer to strike again, the stone splits in two before one word ever leaves your mouth.

Isaiah 65:24 – "And it shall come to pass, that before they call, I will answer; and while they are yet speaking, I will hear."

In Luke 18: 1-8, Jesus uses this parable to stress the importance of perseverance. While this is not a comparison between God and the unjust judge but a contrast, He nevertheless uses this parable to stress the importance of being a stonecutter. The power of contrast is used to highlight differences and not similarities. Black ink on snow white paper shows the contrast between the two, so this is a parable that contrasts God with the unjust judge.

The widow in the story was a stonecutter. Even though this was not a real widow or judge, Jesus knew that His audience was very familiar with widows and judges like this. Let us look at this parable and see what motivated this stonecutter to strike at this judge's stony heart.

It is important to note that widows in Jesus' day were often the poorest of the poor. They were not guaranteed their husbands' inheritance when he died, as most often, it went to a male family member. Widows were often not even certain of where they would live. Their gender and the culture was against them, but their greatest opponent was poverty. Many widows just accepted it. They never struck the stone of the status quo, but the widow in this story was different. There are things going on in your life and you have accepted it because you feel that you are at its mercy.

"You are never at the mercy of people or circumstances as long as you can pray." – Michael Canion

This widow said to herself, *I know the system is against me, but my need is too great to accept this. I am desperate for change.* Her desperation fueled her desire to persevere and strike against the system. But after making the decision to do something, she has to get an audience with the judge and hope that he will avenge her of her adversary. So, she goes to the judge and he is the worst of the worst. He does not fear God nor regard man. He cares nothing about justice or mercy. She was seemingly at the mercy of a hard-hearted, unjust judge, but in reality, she was not at his mercy; he was at hers.

It is important to note that during those times, the judge was a circuit judge. He would go from place to place and under his tent, he would listen to complaints and make a decision. They were known for being dishonest and most times to get justice, you had to have bribe money. This widow had no money and no connections to anyone who did. But what she had made up for what she did not have, she had a stonecutter's heart. We must develop a stonecutter's heart, a heart to keep coming and striking at things so hard that many a hammer had been broken against it. But what really drove this stonecutting widow? She was driven by a great need and that need fueled her passion and perseverance. Throughout the Bible, we see that the presence of need drove men and women to seek Jesus, whether it was the ten lepers who needed healing, Bartimaeus who needed his sight or the woman with the issue of blood who needed her flow to stop. This widow was another person who joined this chorus of need and she felt deeply about what she needed. When you feel deeply, it fuels your passion for change.

In nothing is this illustrated more clearly than when it comes to parents praying for their children to change. All across this nation and the world, parents take their children before God in prayer because of their passion to see a change in their children. Alone with God, they pour out their heart with strong tears asking God to save and deliver their children. There is little passion that can compare to that of a parent praying for their child.

"You cannot pray passionately unless you feel deeply."
– *Michael Canion*

The prayers of parents are filled with passion, power and perseverance because the child occupies such a prominent place in the heart and it is the heart that reaches out to God. The heart is the hand of the soul that reaches out to God. You cannot truly pray without the heart because the heart is what finds its way to God. Praying is a matter of the heart. Jairus was wealthy and well-respected, but when his daughter was near death, he came in all his pomp and expensive clothes and fell at Jesus' feet. What people thought about him didn't matter. How much he paid for his clothes didn't matter. His position didn't matter. What mattered was that his daughter was dying and there was one man who could save her. He fell at Jesus' feet as a man dying of thirst would fall at a water brook. His heart lay prostrate long before his body ever touched the ground because it was his heart that reached out to Jesus. The heart of Jairus reached out and touched the heart of Jesus and Jesus saw that his heart was ripe for a miracle. Many parents are in a fierce battle for their children, but remember "The battle rages fiercest where there is much to be gained."

Parents pray again and again because of what's at stake. Every time the parent prays, a strike is made. I say to every parent that your prayers are weakening the stone of your children's heart and loosening the grip of the enemy, even though you don't see any evidence. You look for evidence of change and see none because our evidence is not perceived, it is possessed. Our evidence is our faith in a prayer answering God.

Hebrews 11:1 – ¹ *Now faith is the substance of things hoped for, the evidence of things not seen.*

One of the definitions of substance in this text is a title deed. A deed is proof of ownership, therefore your faith is the proof that your child will be saved. Every time the enemy tempts you to doubt, remind yourself that you have proof.

Every day you rise, strike, knowing that one day, one blow will crack that stony heart and they will come to God on their knees with hands raised.

The widow in our text saw this judge as being her only hope, so she refused to stop striking at his heart. To her, he was her only hope, even though she had no reason to hope in him. She just kept striking at his heart. There are times when we, like Abraham, must hope against hope. We must expect something positive in our future, even though our situation presents a formidable case against it.

She struck at his heart when he went shopping. She struck at his heart when he was with friends. She struck at his heart while he was walking to the bathroom. She struck in the wee hours of the night, saying, "Avenge me of my adversary." She struck so often that he got no rest. The passionate person strikes even though the hammer must be taped to his hands because his hands are too weary from striking to maintain its grip.

She continued to strike at his heart at different times of the day and this is what it means to always pray. To always pray means to continue to bring the same thing before the Lord. It does not mean to repetitiously say the same thing over and over again. To always pray means to regularly bring your petition before God. If you are passionate about the petition, lay before the Lord and bring it often.

In Luke 18:4-5, we read, [4] And he would not for a while: but afterward he said within himself, Though I fear not God, nor regard man; [5] Yet because this widow troubleth me, I will avenge her, lest by her continual coming she weary me.

The point is that by her continually striking she broke the hard heart of an unjust judge.

The contrast is stated in Luke 18:6-7 , [6] And the Lord said, Hear what the unjust judge saith. [7] And shall not God avenge his own elect, which cry day and night unto him, though he bear long with them?

If this widow can get justice from an unjust judge, how much more can we get from a just God who is our Father and who is ready to avenge us, whose prayers strike before Him day and night?

In my life, there were things that I prayed for until I became weary. I continued to strike at my situation with prayer and yet, nothing seemed to be happening. Rather than do what Jesus taught in this parable, I became disappointed and depressed. Sometimes, it is not just the presence of the trial alone that presents the challenge; it is the longevity of it. When you have been praying, hoping and fighting for a long period of time, the longevity of the trial has the potential to rob you of your willingness to strike again. But, you must strike because you are a stonecutter. When prayer seems to fail, it only *seems* that way. We may not get what we want, when we want it or how we expect it to come, but prayer never fails.

3

No Mind To Pray

"Therefore, whether the desire to pray be on you or not, get to your closet at a set time, shut yourself in with God; wait upon Him; seek His face; realize Him; pray."
– R.F. Horton

*Luke 18:1 – Then Jesus told his disciples a parable to show them that they should always pray and **not give up**.*

Personally, I went through a period when I became weary in my mind. My heart was overwhelmed and it seemed as though my prayers went no further than the ceiling. Mentally, I was beginning to move away from prayer and toward depression. I did not move from there overnight; it was a process of compromising my devotional time and it was slow and ever so subtle. Subtlety has the ability to dull your senses to the change. Subtlety is one of the greatest weapons in the arsenal of the enemy; he seems to believe that the slow way is the best way.

So slow was the process that when I realized the condition I was in, I said, "How did I get in this shape?" The hour hand on a clock moves so slowly that you don't really notice it. All you know is that it continues to get a lot closer to the next number. It is possible with a highly sensitive dimmer switch to dim the lights in a room so slowly that you can find yourself in darkness without knowing when the lights finally turn off. I was allowing compromise brought on by depression to take me from the closet and in doing so, I became vulnerable to the attacks of the enemy.

I have gone through tremendous highs and debilitating lows in the school of prayer. There were periods when in my depression, there was just no mind to pray. You will not find the word "depression" in the Bible. Instead, the Bible uses words like downcast, sad, discouraged, downhearted and miserable. The Bible is replete with instances of people who suffered from depression, such as Naomi, Ruth, David, King Solomon and Jeremiah, to name a few.

"I find myself frequently depressed, perhaps more than any other person here. And I find no better cure for that depression than to trust in the Lord with all my heart and seek to realize afresh the peace speaking blood of Jesus, and His infinite love in dying upon the cross to put away all my transgressions." – Charles Spurgeon

Elijah the prophet defeated the false prophets of Baal on Mount Carmel, but instead of being encouraged, Elijah, fearing Jezebel, was afraid. 1 Kings 19:4-5 describes what he did. "He came to a bush, sat down under a tree and prayed that he might die. 'I have had enough, LORD,' he said. 'Take my life; I am no better than my ancestors.' Then he lay down under the bush and fell asleep."

Elijah didn't really want to die because Jezebel would have been happy to oblige him.

While in the grip of depression, you may say things you really don't mean. You are speaking out of your pain and God knows it. How many people have said, "Lord I'm tired. I can't take it anymore. If You are not going to fix this situation, then just take me home." If God had listened every time people said that, there would have been a mass exodus.

"The Christian life is not a constant high. I have my moments of deep discouragement. I have to go to God in prayer with tears in my eyes and say, 'O God, forgive me,' or 'Help me.'" – Billy Graham

Depression can get so bad that you seemingly refuse to be comforted. It's almost as though we embrace the depression. There was a pastor I knew who was so depressed and so discouraged that when he was encouraged to pray, he quickly retorted, "You pray." He was speaking out of his depression, out of his pain because prayer seemed to fail him.

The spirit of depression had gripped me until I had no mind and no energy to pray. It seemed as though prayer had failed me. It seemed that God did not care. I believed in what could happen through prayer, but I had a great deal of doubt as to whether it would happen for me. I would walk by the designated place of prayer in our house and glance in that direction, too ashamed to look directly at it because I should have been in there. It was as though God was waiting on me to come, but I did not keep the appointment. I did not come to Him, yet He prayed for me and He prays for you, as well.

"If I could hear Christ praying for me in the next room, I would not fear a million enemies. Yet distance makes no difference. He is praying for me." – Robert Murray McCheyne

I praise and honor God for every attribute He possesses, but I thank Him more than I can ever articulate with words for His Mercy, for in His mercy, He gives us what we need and not what we deserve. I was so depressed that the only thing I could say was, "Lord, have mercy on me." Small problems loomed large and larger problems seemed insurmountable. It is interesting that when a pastor is in the midst of depression, most people don't really know it. There are those who are close to you that maybe sense that something is not quite right, but they are accustomed to you showing up every week, encouraging everyone with a smile on your face. There are many wounded, hurting and depressed men and women of God who are given enough grace to serve only to get by themselves and be crushed by the weight of depression. Depression was crushing me. I felt hopeless, but I just would not run to the closet and shut myself in with God.

It was during this time that, from my perspective, the bottom fell out. One Sunday morning, while preparing for church, one of the deacons called me. He said, "Bishop, the power is off at the church." I was already in a bad place and this pushed me even further into it. I was dumbfounded because even though giving had declined due to the economy being in such a bad state, I knew that we had paid the power bill. This was the last thing I needed. As it turned out, the bill had been paid. However, we paid it based on our monthly average, but the bill was about sixty dollars more than normal. We were told that they would just roll it into the next bill. Later, we found out that we had been given misinformation. We could have easily paid the sixty dollars, but decided to just pay it with the following bill. This was a huge mistake. Now, on top of the depression, I was scrambling to get the power on. We paid the bill immediately, but this was Sunday morning and they could give us no definite time as to when the power would be on. The first thing that came to my mind was, *What will the people think if the power is not on at the time of the morning service?* The power was not turned on until late that evening.

It just so happened that I had received a generator as a gift the previous year. I rushed to the church with it and found the deacons walking around, getting flashlights and candles. We connected the generator and set up in the fellowship hall. We had light, but no microphone or anything else. As people arrived, they wondered, as well they should, what was going on. I felt as though I was under a microscope and everyone was looking at me. I did not have the luxury at that moment of feeling sorry for myself; I had to function because something had to be done. I had everyone stop what they were doing and called them together. I explained what happened, but in my heart, I did not know if anyone believed me or not. It was only by God's grace that I got through the service and we really had a great service, but I was in a bad place emotionally when I arrived at church and a worse place when I left. I thank God for those who loved us and believed the truth concerning what I said and rallied around us. When I left church, I was emotionally done.

I read a book once called, "Dark Threads the Weaver Needs." The premise of the book is that God uses all of the threads of your life to make the pattern He desires. Woven throughout the fabric of your life are dark threads, along with brighter colored ones, but in the sovereignty of God, He uses it all. Sometimes, it may appear that the dark threads are used far too often, but appearances can be deceiving. I was in a dark place, but He used it all to position me and bring my heart back to His. There are no wasted experiences in your walk with God, as long as you learn something from them. Whatever you go through, make sure you come out with something you learned. Don't let it be for nothing.

I also made the tragic mistake of connecting my sense of self-worth to the church. As the church struggled, I struggled. I did not understand why God did not help me.

"I use to ask God to help me. Then I asked if I might help Him. I ended up asking him to do His work through me." – Hudson Taylor

He was helping me all along, only in a way that I could not or perhaps would not understand. Sometimes, we want the kind of help we want and not the kind He decides to give. God has a course for each of us; we must embrace the course and stay on it. The apostle Paul was used mightily by God and many miracles were done through him. That was his course.

John the Baptist never performed one miracle that I have read about. He lived in the wilderness, ate locusts and wild honey and that was his course. But, Jesus said of John the Baptist, "Verily I say unto you, Among them that are born of women there hath not risen a greater than John the Baptist: notwithstanding he that is least in the kingdom of heaven is greater than he" *Matthew 11:11 (KJV)*.

The blinders on a horse keep him free from peripheral distractions. We must have blinders on and stay the course, even when we don't understand the course. As Paul said in *2 Timothy 4:7,* "I have fought a good fight, I have finished *my* course, I have kept the faith. You have a course and I have a course. Whatever your course, embrace it and be the best you can be as you travel it. I believe that God is working something in us by way of the course He carries us.

I did not realize that He was always there helping me and working His plan for my life. Peter rebuked Jesus because He did not understand that Jesus had a predetermined course for His life. He did not understand that the death, burial and resurrection of Jesus was all a part of God's great and wonderful plan, but it was not a part of Peter's plan. Peter was looking for a one kind of Savior, but God sent a Savior of a different kind.

Have you ever been looking for one kind of help and God sent help of another kind and since it was not the kind you were looking for, you did not recognize it when it came? God is working His plan for your life trust Him. Don't become a prisoner of logic because of the things you cannot understand. There are times when He defies logic and chooses for you the course of greatest resistance in order to develop, strengthen and teach you. Regardless of the course, we must trust Him with the outcome. After all, it is the outcome that counts. God has said to me many times, "Trust Me with the outcome."

My wife is a gifted decorator. When it comes to decorating, she just sees things that I don't see. There have been times when she says what she wants to do and I just don't see it. Even while it's coming together, I don't see it, but when I see the outcome, it all makes sense. I have learned to trust her with the outcome when it comes to decorating and I am learning to trust God with the outcome as He works in my life.

In the early stages of the Russian space program, when they returned to Earth after weeks in space, they were barely able to walk and were in generally poor health. In the weightless environment of space, their muscles were not forced to work, so when they returned to Earth, they suffered from atrophy, which is the weakening of the muscles from a lack of use. To combat the problem, they invented something they called a Penguin Suit. This suit was basically a jogging suit with elastic bands throughout it. The bands resisted their every movement, forcing the muscles to be engaged. The resistance supplied by the bands kept the muscles strong. God has bands that He uses to develop and strengthen us for the purpose He has called us. The reality is that without the presence of these bands that cause us to struggle, there would be no strength. We would suffer from spiritual atrophy. The muscles of the weightlifter are a testimony to the ability of struggle to strengthen and develop. Weightlifting is a struggle between the man and the metal. You are stronger. I am stronger. We all are stronger because of our struggles. We can find little if anything positive while we are in the struggle. Most often, the benefits are not seen immediately, but progressively.

This is what Jesus was saying in the garden of Gethsemane when He said, "If it is possible, let this cup pass from Me." He followed that request with, "Nevertheless, not My will but Thy will be done." We all must get to the place of nevertheless. As we travel our course and do not understand His ways, we too must say, "Nevertheless, not my will, but Thy will be done." I struggled because there were things I wanted Him to do and He was doing something else. It seemed as though prayer did not help. In retrospect, I was really trying to get God to agree with what I wanted to do. It was as though I was trying to force my will on God and just in case you don't know, that does not work.

My spirit became dry and parched by the sun of adversity. My unwillingness to stay in His presence and trust the course that He has for my life kept me shackled in depression. I was in a spiritual desert. There was, however, something good that came from being trapped in that spiritual desert. Every day I was there, my spirit's thirst for God grew. You see, there are levels of thirst that you can live with. It may be uncomfortable, but you can live with. But when the dryness of the spirit has reached its peak and you cannot live any longer without water, it is at that point that you begin to pant after God. And that's what happened to me.

Psalm 42:1-2 (KJV) – [1] As the hart panteth after the water brooks, so panteth my soul after thee, O God. [2] My soul thirsteth for God, for the living God: when shall I come and appear before God?

It was no longer about what I wanted Him to do or thought He should have done. Now, in this desert place, I just longed for Him. I sought Him, I sought His heart and not His hand.

Jeremiah 29:13 – You will seek Me and find Me when you seek Me with all your heart.

If you ask a man who is dying of thirst what he desires most, he will not say a house, a car or money; he will say water because he needs water to survive. This spiritual condition would drive me to say water. All of the things I thought I needed Him to do were a non-issue. I needed water. I wanted water and the only way to get it was in God's presence. Some of you reading this book need water. You are weary, depressed and burned out. Only Christ can give the water that quenches your thirsty soul. It is my hope that today will be that day your soul will be refreshed.

I came to realize that from God's perspective, it was never really about the church then, nor is it about the church now; it was always about me – making me, breaking me, teaching me and bringing me to a higher degree of conformity to Christ. I have not arrived, but I am further along in this journey. I think that one of the greatest tragedies today is that few of our prayers have to do with being conformed to the image of Christ. We want to do what Jesus did, but we rarely live as He lived.

There is always a greater purpose connected to what you are going through. Look at Joseph, for instance. What he went through was not really about him, it was about a nation. God was positioning Joseph for His people. Sometimes, we become so consumed with what is going on in our world that we forget that we are character actors and Jesus is the star in a much larger drama.

I was broken and in my brokenness, I had come to grips with my desperate need for revival. In the bible Myrrh is a chalky substance that when broken gives off a sweet aroma. I can now see so clearly the hand of God directing the orchestra of my life. He used every failure, every tear, every fear, every time I was despondent and discouraged. He used it all to teach me more about myself, more about Himself and more about who He wanted me to become.

It was because of the course God took me that I learned to pray. He taught me how to pray and what it means to pray. He revealed to me what a privilege it is to be invited to have an audience with Him. I think it is safe to say that there are things I would not have learned had I not been for the course He has carried and continues to carry me.

I don't profess to be an expert on the subject of prayer because I am not. However, I have learned some practical and insightful things about it. If there are things you can use, use it. If not, disregard it. One of the lessons I learned is that praying is not always about having a mind to do it because there are times when the man does not have the mind.

"Therefore, whether the desire to pray be on you or not, get to your closet at a set time, shut yourself in with God; wait upon Him; seek His face; realize Him; pray."
– R.F. Horton

If you obey the mind when it says not to pray, you disregard the spiritual law that we ought always to pray. The mind is either a powerful ally or an equally powerful adversary when it comes to prayer. This is why the enemy attacks the mind of the saint. Satan and your flesh use every tactic and weapon available to infiltrate your mind and get you to rise from your knees. He targets the mind because as the mind goes, so does the man. He whispers to us that prayer does not help and God does not care. He is the master of suggestive manipulation. All of these are his attempts to pull the mind from the closet. He knows that if we do not pray, we become prey.

The enemy targets the mind and seeks to influence us to think about everything we feel God has not done or is not doing. The more we think on it, the more the mind moves from the closet. He says the closet is a place of wasted time. I was thinking myself away from prayer. Rather than being thankful for the many things God had done, my thoughts were filled with negativity, despair and what He had not done. I was a prisoner of my own thinking and seemingly did not have the mind to escape.

The enemy wants to use your mind against you to keep you from the closet. He wants you to agree with him that prayer is a waste of time. He knows that if he is to be successful, your mind must participate. His preoccupation with keeping us out of the closet begs the question, why is he so concerned that we not go there?

"No one is a firmer believer in the power of prayer than the devil; not that he practices it, but he suffers from it." – Guy H. King

Therein lies the reason for the all-out assault on your mind. Every time we pray, we strike a blow against his kingdom, so he targets our emotions through our minds. He knows that your emotional state is directly linked to your thinking. You are discouraged because of your thinking. You are sad because of your thinking. You are angry because of your thinking. You are depressed because of your thinking. The enemy wants you to dwell on everything that is wrong in your life and then, he whispers, *God has done nothing.*

He is a salesman, peddling his goods and targeting the minds of the saints.

He targeted my mind and tempted me to think on every negative and depressive thing in my life and I did. I was being tempted to move away from the closet and the enemy knows that mental participation is necessary for the success of any temptation.

I allowed him to take advantage of the power of my mind. The mind can take you on a journey to a place you've never been or revisit a place you have. You can be at church and yet, see yourself at home, opening the refrigerator door. As the inside light comes on, you reach for that big glass of cold lemonade. You raise the glass to your mouth and take a drink. If you think hard enough, you can almost feel your jaws twinge from the sour taste of the lemons. You went home without ever leaving the church. It was all done in your mind because you meditated on it. While your body may not have been refreshed by the lemonade you drank, your mind, nevertheless, went through the mental motions.

Has someone ever mistreated you and you brushed it off? Later, when you really thought on what they did, you got angry. The more you meditated on it, the angrier you got. That anger is the result of what you chose to meditate on. Your emotional state is directly linked to the object of your meditation. My emotional state was directly linked to my thoughts, therefore, as my thoughts went, so went my emotions.

It is amazing how at peace you can be until you start thinking about bills, what someone said or who doesn't like you. You can go from peaceful to pathetic all because the object of your meditation changed. These things were there before you began to meditate on them, but it didn't affect you emotionally until after you began to meditate on them. There is nothing good that will result from bad thinking and my thinking was bad.

Most often, when you make the wrong choices, it is because you are thinking about the wrong thing. My thinking was wrong. Depression is the result of the mind's unwillingness to let go of the negative and cling to the positive.

Isaiah 26:3 – "Thou wilt keep him in perfect peace whose mind is stayed in thee."

I had no peace because my mind wandered away from the closet, away from God. Again, in Luke 18:1, we read, "And he spake a parable unto them *to this end*, that men ought always to pray, and not to faint."

Why did Jesus feel it necessary to say this? He knew that we would face the temptation to feel as though praying was a waste of time and if you succumb, you would have no mind to pray. As I went through these depressive phases, I surrendered to that temptation. One thing I learned is that when you have no mind and no desire to pray, go to the closet anyway. Go there, sit there, wrestle there, bring your doubts there if you must, but go. The closet is the environment where desire can rise in the heart and strength can be renewed. This is why it is so important to just be with Him. He knows our frame. He knows our weakness. He helps us in our infirmities.

Romans 8:26-27 – [26] *Likewise the Spirit also helpeth our infirmities: for we know not what we should pray for as we ought: but the Spirit itself maketh intercession for us with groanings which cannot be uttered.* [27] *And he that searcheth the hearts knoweth what is the mind of the Spirit, because he maketh intercession for the saints according to the will of God.*

You may not have the mind, but go to the closet. You may not have the words, but go to the closet. You may not feel worthy, but go there, sit in silence and wait on Him. In your silence, you are much closer to God than you think because your time with Him is not skewed by insincere and selfish words. God understands the language of the heart.

"Sometimes when your child talks, your friends cannot understand what he says; but the mother understands very well. So if our prayer comes from the heart, God understands our language." – D.L. Moody

In our age of much noise, there is little appreciation for silence, there is this seeming addiction to noise. We have no shortage of noise from television, radio, CDs, DVDs, mp3s and cell phones. We have televisions on that we are not even watching, but our addiction to noise is being satisfied, so we leave it on. Silence, however, can be a midwife that helps give birth to a praying heart. If God has you in a place of silence, perhaps He is in the process of birthing something in you.

"The fruit of silence is prayer. The fruit of prayer is faith. The fruit of faith is love. The fruit of love is service. The fruit of service is peace." – Mother Teresa

Never neglect the closet because the desire to be there is absent. Come to Him and wait on Him. "They that wait upon Him shall renew their strength". Short wait or long, wait upon Him, strength and desire will come. The blessing is that prayer is not dependent on us alone, we have help. He just wants us to be there. If we wait in His presence , He changes us. He changes our mind and our manner and we begin to think and act like Him. I needed His presence to change me.

"The Presence of the Father will influence the child who is willing to spend unhurried time with Him." – Unknown

The Power of Presence
I was blessed to have a tremendous father. When I was a child, I wanted to be with my father all day, every day. Whether he was going to his shop or fishing, I wanted to be there. Being in his presence impacted me. I found that the more I was with him, the more I became like him. There are things I do today and the only reason I do them is because I saw my father do

them an. Being with him affected my mind and mannerisms. When he had a headache, he took a certain brand of pain reliever and today, I have the same brand in my cabinet. He walked with a slight limp. As a child, I started walking with a slight limp because my father did it and I wanted to do it. My father's life and presence had and still has a great impact on me. I needed time in my heavenly Father's presence so that He could change me.

Got my Mind Back

When I could take it no more, my thirst for God became unbearable. My thirst for a change was so great, it transcended both the discouragement and depression. I had to spend unhurried time with God, so I went to the closet and fell to my knees. I had no words to say, but I knew I had to be with God. I knew I needed change and He was the only One who could help me and I was determined to stay there, no matter how long it took. I knelt down and was silent. The silence was both quiet and deafening at the same time, but I was there. Finally in the presence of God, I could finally exhale. For the Christian, "Prayer is the air we breathe and if we don't pray, we suffocate, but when we do, we exhale." I had been suffocating from prayerlessness brought on by a depressed spirit, but now I could breathe and there, alone with God, the tears began to swell and I cried. I was in a safe place to break.

I said no words, but my tears and the anguish of my soul said it all. In the 30th chapter of 1Samuel, David cried until he had no power to cry anymore. In that moment, I could identify with him. It was as though my very soul had been weeping before God. Men generally have two types of cries

31

and specific places to cry. In public, no matter how deeply a man hurts, he will strain not to cry aloud. Tears may swell, but in his heart, he is saying to himself, "Whatever you do, don't cry." He must be dignified.

However, there is another cry that a man will do when the pain is unbearable; I call it the ugly cry. It is a cry that is both loud and passionate. It is the cry of the soul. It is the cry that has no concern for who is watching. The face is contorted, the eyes are squinted and the tears flow like a river from a dam that just broke. In the presence of God, I felt safe and my soul began to cry to Him. In this secret place, I was with my Father. He did not think less of me. To Him, I was no less a man because of the depth of my pain, nor the anguish of my tears. I did not have to wear a facade; I could be free to hurt.

When I had no more tears, my heart began to reach for Him and I said, "Help me." As I continued to call out to Him, I felt His presence so strongly that I don't have an adequate vocabulary to describe it. His presence to me was like a salve to my wounded soul. I called out to Him and He heard me. Everything I had been through – every discouragement, every tear and every bit of that stifling depression – was worth it if that is what it took to bring me to this moment. In that moment, His presence changed me.

"There is a place of such communion with God where time is a non-issue, every moment has a majesty all its own. It is only tempered by the knowledge that it has to end" – Michael Canion

4

The Act of Praying

"The act of praying is a combination of things that occur during the time you devote to Him. The operative word is time because prayer cannot happen without time. Whether the time is short or long there is no prayer without time. God waits every day for us to spend time, unhurried time with Him."

Matthew 6:5-6 (NASB) – [5] *"When you pray, you are not to be like the hypocrites; for they love to stand and pray in the synagogues and on the street corners so that they may be seen by men. Truly I say to you, they have their reward in full.* [6] *But you, when you pray, go into your inner room, close your door and pray to your Father who is in secret, and your Father who sees what is done in secret will reward you."*

Jesus said when you pray, when deals with time, the time with God however is composed of many things. Prayer is petition. Prayer is silence. Prayer is asking. Prayer is thanksgiving. Prayer is worship. Prayer is supplication. Prayer is intercession. Prayer is meditation. Prayer is travailing. The world dictionary defines prayer as a "personal communication or petition addressed to a deity, especially in the form of supplication, adoration, praise, contrition or thanksgiving."

During the time you spend with a person, there are many components that comprise the time you spend with him. You ask. You listen. You ponder. You may thank them for something they did. You may give them something. They may ask you for something. They may tell you something. You may celebrate a particular attribute of theirs. The point is that during the time you spend with them there are a number of things that make up the time.

Likewise prayer, which again is basically time spent with God, is multifaceted. We must be careful that it does not simply become a habit that is void of any power because we focus on a part without realizing its relationship to the whole, and its goal of developing intimacy with God.

Each of these things may happen at different times during your time with God because each time with Him carries both similarities and differences. Don't be guilty of trying to make a part fit during a time when it doesn't. Sometimes, when you begin your time with Him, the spirit of thanksgiving is prevalent in your heart. Offer thanksgiving and don't feel like you must petition first or be silent first. Let each time with Him determine how you spend it. While it is good to have a plan, it must be a plan that is subject to change.

"The more I pray, the more I come to realize that the greater part of prayer is to be with God. More than

what we say is the fact that we are with Him. Just be with Him..." – Michael Canion

During the time we spend with Him, we must engage the mind to think on God and realize that He is present. When His presence cannot be perceived with the senses, we must know He is there. There must be the realization that He is closer than near to me – He is here with me. When you talk to a friend or relative, your senses can perceive their presence. You can see them, hear them or touch them. We must know that God is present because He said He would be with us. You and I must believe in whom we cannot see.

John 20:27-29 (KJV) – [27] Then saith he to Thomas, Reach hither thy finger, and behold my hands; and reach hither thy hand, and thrust it into my side: and be not faithless, but believing. [28] And Thomas answered and said unto him, My Lord and my God. [29] Jesus saith unto him, Thomas, because thou hast seen me, thou hast believed: blessed are they that have not seen, and yet have believed.

Jesus pronounces those blessed who believe and have not seen. He is present with us, however, that does not mean that it is a reality to us. Is His presence real to you?

There is a dual aspect of presence. He is present with us on one hand and we must be present with Him on the other. What I mean by that is you must be there in the moment with God, emotionally and mentally. The mind can wander away from God with the speed of a two-year-old on caffeine or it can move toward Him with the speed of a snail in slow motion.

"The battle of prayer is against two things in the earthlies, wondering thoughts and lack of intimacy with God's character as revealed in His word; neither can be cured at once but can be cured by discipline." – Oswald Chambers

The mind can so easily wander while trying to pray and sometimes, you don't even know you've drifted until you catch yourself and ask yourself, "What am I thinking?" Your body can be kneeling, but your mind can be running to bills you owe, what someone said or perhaps a project you are working on. Our minds will run in the direction of whatever is the priority of the moment and there are other times where you have no idea why you are thinking about some things. It is a blessing indeed to be able to stay in the moment with God.

We cannot honor God with our mouths when our minds don't even know what was said because it was elsewhere. There have been times when I knelt to pray and my mind had drifted so far from Him that when I came to myself, I felt like a straight heathen. I'm on my knees, but when my mind drifts to a football game or something that happened or appears likely to happen, I feel so unspiritual. But, I think this is all part of this process of learning to focus, so just stay on point and pray. No matter how many times you drift, keep coming back because it does get better as you go and grow.

A kneeling body must have a kneeling mind in order to be in the moment with God. Whether you pray for fifteen minutes or an hour, be there. Prayer is a body composed of many parts and these parts make up the whole of the time you devote to God.

5

What is Prayer?

"Prayer is an expression of my need to depend on God."

Psalm 50:15 – "And call upon me in the day of trouble: I will deliver thee, and thou shalt glorify me."

Prayer, more than anything, is how we express our need of God. We pray because we are insufficient of ourselves. If we had no need, we would not pray. We are limited, vulnerable and needy on so many levels that we must pray.

When my daughter was about four, she illustrated prayer by something she did on Father-Daughter day. On Father-Daughter day, we would spend the day together and on this particular day, we went to a certain store. When we arrived and began to walk toward the store, she held my hand tightly, like a prayer. This was an expression of her need and her dependence on me. I will never forget how tightly she held my hand and by doing so, she spoke volumes without saying a word. The pressure she applied articulated a message that her limited vocabulary could not. Her tiny fingers conveyed an unspoken prayer as she wrapped them around my finger.

She communicated so much by her language of touch that words were unnecessary, for she spoke in a universal language that I understood. Children speak in a language that may be foreign to others, yet the parent knows all too well what the child says. Without opening her mouth, she said, "I need you." Sometimes, you have no words, but your Father knows.

She did not hold my hand loosely, as though my presence was a luxury. She was keenly aware that my presence was not to be taken for granted. As we walked, she held my hand and I held hers.

Isaiah 41:13 says, "For I the Lord thy God will hold thy right hand, saying unto thee, Fear not; I will help thee." The holding of a hand is a language all its own. When a husband holds the hand of his wife, it conveys many things that both understand. When we shake the hand of an acquaintance, it expresses the pleasure we feel from being blessed by their presence. When we speak of holding onto God's hand, it speaks of a child holding the hand of his Father. How tightly we hold His hand reveals how deeply we recognize our need. How often or seldom we pray reveals the degree to which we feel we need to reach for Him and prayer is the hand of the heart that reaches up to God.

Her need of me was also expressed by her proximity to my right leg. She wanted to be as close to me as possible. Apparently, she realized that there is safety in intimacy. There were times I walked closely to God because I knew how much I needed Him. There were other times I walked at a distance because I felt as though I could handle it. Any stroll you take where God at a distance is a dangerous walk. We may not have verbally said that we didn't need Him, but our actions say what our mouths do not.

The closer my daughter walked to me, the better she felt. Her courage was connected to my presence. Her safety was connected to my presence. When I stopped, she stopped. When I slowed, she slowed. Her willingness to proceed was connected to my willingness to lead. She would go no further than I went, nor walk any faster than I walked.

How often have we willed ourselves to move forward when divine stop signs flashed in our spirits like neon lights against the backdrop of a blanket of darkness? How often have you willingly disobeyed God, choosing rather to gratify the flesh and make light of your disobedience? As I was going through my depression, I could sense God calling me to the closet, but I would not come. I would not say yes.

Bishop Charles Mason sang a song that came to be the anthem for the denomination. The song was, "Yes Lord." This praise was born out of the heart of a man whose will became submissive to the will of God through intimate fellowship with God. In prayer, you learn to say yes.

As we approached the sidewalk, I could feel her fingers began to loosen. Once we reached the sidewalk, clear of any foreseeable danger, the little fingers that once held my hand so tightly released my hand altogether. Once again, she was speaking, but the message was quite different. Holding my hand tightly expressed the depth of her need. Holding my hand loosely expressed the presence of a need that was not as deep. Releasing my hand altogether expressed the absence of a need. It was an external expression of an internal conclusion. The conclusion was that she could handle it from here.

Sometimes, either the longevity or intensity of the struggle or the ease and comfort of life can influence us to loosen our grip. Two completely different reasons that yield the same result, distance between you and God.

Once we stepped onto the sidewalk, she became a victim of her desire for independence. I could feel her pulling away and with every pull, she was saying, "Let me go." How many times have our actions said the same thing to God when there was something we wanted to do? How many times have out actions said to God, "Let me go?"

I went from leader to follower because her opinion of her neediness had changed. When she was confident that she no longer needed me, she took upon herself a role for which she was not qualified: the role of leader. This ever so slight change in geography gave her a feeling of security, confidence and control. Once we stepped onto the sidewalk, she felt confident. She failed to realize that she was just as needy walking on the sidewalk as she was crossing the parking lot. Suddenly, a young lady exited the store pushing a buggy. Momentarily, the buggy was coming towards her and she felt threatened. In an instant, she hurried to my side, gripped my hand and regained the posture she had maintained prior to being convinced that she no longer needed me. The perception of being safe and secure lulls us into a false sense of security and causes us to believe that our need is not as deep as it actually is.

There are times we feel so helpless, hopeless and afraid that we are motivated to cleave to God as my daughter cleaved to me. But, the moment we feel as though we have some degree of control, we begin to leave instead of cleave.

Uzziah, the Seeking and Needy King
In II Chronicles, we read that King Uzziah began his reign when he was sixteen years old. Imagine the awesome responsibility of a kingdom being placed on the shoulders of a sixteen-year-old. For Uzziah, however, youth and inexperience seemed to have been an asset. The awareness of his insufficiency for the task at hand possibly caused him to recognize his need to depend on God. II Chronicles 26:5 reads, "And he sought God in the days of Zechariah, who had understanding in the visions of God: and as long as he sought the Lord, God made him to prosper." Uzziah sought God and found Him.

Deuteronomy 4:29 reads, "But if from thence thou shalt seek the Lord thy God, thou shalt find him, if thou seek him with all thy heart and with all thy soul."

If we do not seek God, it is because we believe we know how, when and what needs to be done. Therefore, we have no need of God's assistance. Often, there is a great gulf between the perception of our need and reality of its depth. Uzziah was needy and inexperienced, but more importantly, he seemed to realize it. Do you really realize how deeply you need God?

Uzziah began his reign with the realization of his need for God, but at some point he lost this realization and it was a prelude to disaster. In 2nd Chronicles 26:15-16 it reads, "And he made in Jerusalem engines, invented by cunning men, to be on the towers and upon the bulwarks, to shoot arrows and great stones withal. And his name spread far abroad; for he was marvelously helped, till he was strong. **But when he was strong, his heart was lifted up to his destruction**: for he transgressed against the Lord his God, and went into the temple of the Lord to burn incense upon the altar of incense."

God gave Uzziah great prosperity and power. Uzziah allowed the blessings to influence him toward pride and away from prayer. The more you walk toward pride, the more you walk away from prayer.

The Bible, in Proverbs 16:18, warns that, "Pride goeth before destruction, and an haughty spirit before a fall."

If God has given you wealth, influence, popularity or power; be thankful and careful. God hates the proud. It is normal for us to feel elated when God accomplishes a certain task through us and oh, how we would love to take the credit. We may often declare phrases that point to God as our source, but these words may not be consistent with what is in our hearts. But, we must remember that, "It is God which worketh in you both to will and to do of his good pleasure" Philippians 2:13. Regardless of your position in society, God expects you to honor, worship and obey Him. For much of his life, Uzziah "did that which was right in the sight of the Lord" 2 Chronicles 26:4,

But, Uzziah eventually became prideful and he was struck with leprosy for the rest of his life. He is remembered more for his pride, arrogance and subsequent punishment than for his great reforms. As long as Uzziah recognized his need to depend on God, God marvelously helped him. The word 'marvelously' comes from a word that means to marvel or be astonished. God is waiting to do things for us and through us that will leave people in awe, but we must be prayerful people and depend on God.

In 2 Chronicles 16:7-9 (Living), we read what Hanani said to King Asa:

"Because you have depended on the king of Syria instead of the Lord your God, the army of the king of Syria has escaped from you. Don't you remember what happened to the Ethiopians and Libyans and their vast army, with all of their chariots and cavalrymen? But you relied then on the Lord, and he delivered them all into your hand. For the eyes of the Lord search back and forth across the whole earth, looking for people whose hearts are perfect toward him, so that he can show his great power helping them. What a fool you have been! From now on you shall have wars."

It is humbling when we consider that the greatest hindrance to manifestations of God's ability is not Satan or the world; it is our own unwillingness to consciously and consistently depend on God.

God is waiting to manifest marvelous help on behalf of those who are aware of how badly they need Him. I think that the degree to which we are affected by sin reveals itself by our constant attempts to act independently of God. How often has God said, "Go left" and you went right? He said, "Be still" and you moved. He said, "No," but you said, "Yes." It is almost as though you are trying to will your choice to be the right one.

My daughter let go of my hand when she reached the sidewalk and I withdrew from the closet when I became depressed. Uzziah withdrew his hand from God's when he became strong, but we do not have the luxury of letting go His hand. Uzziah was deceived into believing that the presence of prosperity and the comfort that it afforded voided his neediness. He did not realize that he was just as needy in his strength as he was in his weakness. He apparently thought that he had outgrown his need to depend on God. During the course of our lives, there are things we will outgrow, however, we will never outgrow our constant need of God.

It may be tempting to believe that your experiences or accomplishments lessen the depth of your need. However, your need is so great and its depth so deep that no words in any language can adequately describe it.

We sometimes venture away from God when we are deceived concerning our need. This deception is rooted in pride, which may be the result of academic achievement, wealth or natural ability. There was an old seasoned preacher who once said, "While preaching my first sermon, I was so nervous that my sweat was sweating. I was scared, insecure and totally dependent on God. My dependence was so great that the Lord blessed me greatly. After many years of preaching, I realize that I am just as needy and dependent on God today as when I preached my first sermon." He realized that the effectiveness of the message lay not in the experience of the messenger, but in the power of his God. You may grow in experience and knowledge, but again, you will never outgrow your need to depend on God, a need that we reveal by praying. We never outgrow the need to depend on Him. We seem to struggle with realizing how absolute our helplessness is in accomplishing His work.

We must draw what we need from God to do what he has called us to do. Jesus said, "Abide in me, and I in you. As the branch cannot bear fruit of itself, except it abide in the vine; no more can ye, except ye abide in me. I am the vine, ye are the branches: He that abides in me, and I in him, the same brings forth much fruit: for without me ye can do nothing" John 15:1-5. To be 'without' means to apart from or severed from. A branch severed from the vine is without the vine.

You and I are without the Vine when we try to be fruitful in our own strength and resources apart from Him. Branches cannot bear fruit apart from the vine because it draws what it needs from the vine in order to fulfill its purpose. In prayer we abide, we draw what we need from God's presence in order to fulfill His purpose for us. I believe that the fulfillment of our purpose is directly related to quality time spent with God. What you and I are called to do can only be done as we depend on Him, prayer is how we express our need to depend on Him.

The moment you change the object of your dependence, you void the power of God and what you do in your own power is a work of the flesh. Abraham and Sarah were guilty of a flesh work when they agreed that Abraham should go unto Hagar. They did not inquire of the Lord because apparently, they felt they didn't need to. In their impatience, they became self-dependent, rather than God-dependent. You were created a dependent being, but you were created to depend on God. When you do not have a relationship of acknowledged dependence on God manifested by prayer, you will find something or someone in whom to depend!

Galatians 4:22-23: "For it is written, that Abraham had two sons, the one by a bondmaid, the other by a freewoman. But he who was of the bondwoman was born after the flesh; but he of the freewoman was by promise."

6

My Need Qualifies Me

"God chooses the unlikely to accomplish the impossible that no flesh should glory." – Michael Canion

2 Corinthians 4:7 – "But we have this treasure in earthen vessels, that the excellency of the power may be of God, and not of us."

I was watching television one day and a commercial came on about an oil additive. This product was reported to make even the worse engine perform better and with more power. To demonstrate the effectiveness of the additive, the people in the commercial went to the junkyard and chose the worst running vehicle they could find. They started the engine and it performed poorly. As a matter of fact, to say that it performed poorly is a generous choice of words. The engine performed as though it had no oil or hope at all. Once the additive was poured in the engine, it performed much better. Why was the engine with the greatest need chosen? The engine with the greatest need was chosen so that the change in performance would be attributed to the additive; it was qualified because of its need. The presence of such a great need afforded the opportunity for an effective demonstration. Everyone's attention was focused not on the engine, but on the power working through it. If a new Corvette had been used, there would have been room for doubt because a Corvette is known for its performance. However, when something or someone performs outside of its ability, attention is drawn to that which powers it. This is why God chose you and me. He chose to manifest His ability through weak and needy vessels like you and me, as we depend on Him. None of us have it all together; God knows it and so do we. It is somewhat strange that what people view as a liability, God sees as a qualifying asset.

I have seen many pictures of what people believe Samson looked like. The pictures that I have seen portray him as a person who is physically intimidating. The only noteworthy physical attribute that I read about concerning Samson was the length of his hair, not his intimidating stature.

Samson may have been about five feet seven inches weighing one hundred fifty-five pounds. It is quite possible that when people saw what Samson could do, they were immediately aware that the strength he demonstrated was not of himself. Therefore, his enemies sought to find the secret of his strength. "And Delilah said to Samson, Tell me, I pray thee, wherein thy great strength lieth, and wherewith thou mightiest be bound to afflict thee" Judges 16:6. If Samson had been mighty in appearance, they would have assumed the source of his strength to be of himself.

I don't think that his physical appearance was, in any way, indicative of a person who performs such feats of strength. It is likely that when they looked at Samson physically, then saw what he could do, they concluded that the power was not of himself. There was a power working through this weak and needy vessel.

Paul said it best when he said, in 2 Corinthians 3:5, "Not that we are sufficient of ourselves to think anything as of ourselves, but our sufficiency is of God."

Again, Paul said, "But we have this treasure in earthen vessels, that the excellency of the power may be of God, and not of us. We are troubled on every side, yet not distressed; we are perplexed, but not in despair; Persecuted, but not forsaken; cast down, but not destroyed" 2 Corinthians 4:7-9.

I think we would like to believe God chose us for a particular area of service because of something that we deemed an asset. God may have chosen you because of your liabilities.

"For ye see your calling, brethren, how that not many wise men after the flesh, not many mighty, not many noble, are called: But God hath chosen the foolish things of the world to confound the wise; and God hath chosen the weak things of the world to confound the things that are mighty; And base things of the world, and things that are despised, hath God chosen, yea, and things which are not, to bring to naught things that are: That no flesh should glory in his presence" 1 Corinthians 1:26-29.

God chooses the weak because it is through our weakness that His strength is made perfect as we pray. We can do nothing without Him. John 15:5 5 says, "I am the vine, ye are the branches: He that abideth in me, and I in him, the same bringeth forth much fruit: for without me ye can do nothing."

If God were to choose a basketball team, He might choose guards that could not dribble, forwards that could not shoot and a center that was five feet five inches tall. He would then take them to the championship and win the game. God uses the unlikely to accomplish the impossible that no flesh should glory.

> *2 Corinthians 12:9-10 – "And he said unto me, My grace is sufficient for thee: for my strength is made perfect in weakness. Most gladly therefore will I rather glory in my infirmities, that the power of Christ may rest upon me. Therefore I take pleasure in infirmities, in reproaches, in necessities, in persecutions, in distresses for Christ's sake: for when I am weak, then am I strong."*

The reason you were chosen necessitates your need to pray and depend on God.

7

I Don't Know What To Do

"We seem only to realize the depth of our need of God when faced with an overwhelming situation. We seek God intensely after we have exhausted all other resources and are still left wanting." – Unknown

2 Chronicles 20:12 – "O our God, wilt thou not judge them? for we have no might against this great company that cometh against us; neither know we what to do: but our eyes are upon thee."

In 2 Chronicles 20, we read that Jehoshaphat was facing a huge army. What does he do? He prays. This prayer resulted from the awareness of his need when confronted by such a great multitude. The awareness of his need is revealed by the statement, "Neither know we what to do, but our eyes are on You." Perhaps he would not have sought God had the enemy been much smaller in number. Small adversaries can be an occasion to become deceived concerning the magnitude of our need. In actuality, no adversary is small when you face it in your own strength. It is not the size of the adversary that determines its might. You make the determination the moment you decide upon whom you will depend: God or self. Who are you really depending on? When you depend on yourself, the smallest adversary instantly manifests in size.

In the book of Joshua, the children of Israel felt confident when they went into battle against Ai because Ai was small in number.

Joshua said unto him, "Let not all the people go up; but let about two or three thousand men go up and smite Ai; and make not all the people to labor thither; for they are but few. So there went up thither of the people about three thousand men: and they fled before the men of Ai. And the men of Ai smote of them about thirty and six men: for they chased them from before the gate even unto Shebarim, and smote them in the going down: wherefore the hearts of the people melted, and became as water." Joshua 7: 3-5

They were defeated miserably by this small army because they went in their own strength. We must realize that the depth of our need is not heightened by the presence of a storm, nor is it lessened by the appearance of calm. The relationship of need and dependence must not be fluctuating but constant.

The songwriter, Annie Hawks, wrote, "I need thee, oh I need thee every hour I need thee." Need and want express two different degrees of desire. Need conveys the intensity and depth of our desire; a desire based on personal awareness of the necessity to depend on God. Want conveys a desire based not on necessity but luxury. You need to depend on God.

You are so needy that you could not come to Jesus on your own. Jesus said, "No man can come to me, except the Father which hath sent me draw him." John 6:44

You don't even know what to pray without the help of the Spirit. "For we know not what we should pray as we ought: but the Spirit himself maketh intercession for us with groaning which cannot be uttered." Romans 8:27

We cannot come to the Lord unless you are drawn. We cannot pray as we ought unless we are helped. Yet, we still seem to struggle with realizing the depth of our need to depend on God.

The Bible, in Proverbs 3:6, says, "In all thy ways acknowledge him, and he shall direct thy paths." This call to acknowledge God in all our ways expresses at least two things. First, it expresses your need to be helped in all things and secondly, it expresses God's willingness to help you in all things. In lieu of our need to be helped in all things, we should all be prayer warriors.

The term 'prayer warrior' should apply to every Christian because the depth of our need does not vary from person to person. We depend on Him because we need Him. If dependence on God was not based on our need, we would probably never seek Him.

When I first joined the military as a seventeen-year-old, every time I got a chance, I was calling home. I was in an unfamiliar environment and that caused me to reach out for the familiar. Each time I called, it was an expression of my need for the familiar. As time passed, the unfamiliar became familiar and I didn't feel as though I needed to call home nearly as much.

My calls became so infrequent that on one occasion, my mother called the company commander to see if I was alright. Needless to say, my company commander was not pleased to hear from my mother. He was very cordial and nice to her, but he let me know in very unsanctified terms that I needed to call home more often. Those of you who have been in the military know what I mean by 'unsanctified terms.' However, there was a time when I got in a little, let's call it "a situation," and I would ring the telephone off the hook because I was in need.

Great need makes prayer warriors and it also made me call home. Need often motivates us to do what we otherwise would not do. Since we are in a position of need and dependence, it guarantees God that He will hear from us. Whether you call Him sooner or later, often or seldom, you will call.

James, the brother of Jesus, was known as a prayer warrior. It is said, 'His knees were as hard as camel's knees because he was so constant in prayer." Prayer is based on one's awareness of his need of God, a need which, by its depth, is awesome.

8

Prayer and the Needy Heart

"Prayer is the result of a heart that is conscious of its need to depend on God. This is why not all words spoken are necessarily prayers prayed because prayer is a matter of the heart." – Michael Canion

2 Chronicles 26:16 – "But when he was strong, his heart was lifted up to his destruction."

You may feel as though God has not heard your prayer when in fact, maybe you have not truly prayed. Vocabulary does not determine Christian prayer. It is the position of the heart that approaches God that is important. Matthew 6:7 says, "When you pray, use not vain repetitions as the heathen do; for they think they shall be heard for their much speaking."

The heart refers to your inner person, who you really are. The heart that approaches God must be one of humility for the humble heart is submissive and receptive to the will of God.

Isaiah 29:13 – "Wherefore the Lord said, Forasmuch as this people draw near to me with their mouth, and with there their lips do honor me, but have removed their heart for from me, and their fear of me is taught by the precept of men."

God wants what you do to be consistent with who you are. This is worship "in truth" because there is agreement between the hands and the heart. Raised hands signify surrender, but in our hearts, we often resist God. Our hands and heart don't agree. David said, in Psalms 51:6, "Behold thou desireth truth in the inward parts, and in the hidden part thou shalt make me to know wisdom."

Satan's sin was the result of what was said inwardly. "For thou has said in thine heart, I will ascend into heaven, I will exalt my throne above the stars of Good, I will sit also upon the mount of the congregation, in the sides of the north: I will ascend above the heights of the clouds; I will be like the most high." Isaiah 14:13-14

Visible displays of honor are not acceptable to God when my actions are not one with my heart; this is hypocritical. "Even so ye also outwardly appear righteous unto men, but within ye are full of hypocrisy and iniquity." Matthew 23:28

A hypocrite uses what he does or says to mask who he is. One of the Greek words for hypocrite means someone who acts out a part in a play. Actors in Greek drama held huge masks over their faces that were painted to represent the character they were playing. What you saw was the character, not the person.

Proverbs 23:6-7 – "Eat thou not the bread of him that hath an evil eye, neither desire thou his dainty meats: For as he thinketh in his heart, so is he: Eat and drink, saith he to thee; but his heart is not with thee."

The hypocrite is the person who masks his real self. He plays a role designed to convince you that he is genuine. When we approach God, we must do so in truth because our hearts are naked before Him.

"Neither is there any creature that is not manifest in his sight: but all things are naked and open to the eyes of him with whom we have to do" Hebrews 4:13.

His knowledge of your nakedness should be a great incentive to be truthful and humility.

Heart Lift
The true test of humility is not during the time in the wilderness but when you reach the land that flows with milk and honey.

"Beware that thou forget not the Lord thy God, in not keeping his commandments, and his judgments and his statutes, which I command thee this day: Lest when thou hast eaten and art full, and has built goodly house, and dwelt therein; And when thy herds and thy flocks multiply, and thy silver and thy gold is multiplied; and all that thy hast is multiplied; Then thine heart be lifted up, and thou forget the LORD thy God, which brought thee forth out of the land of Egypt, from the house of bondage" Deuteronomy 8:11-14.

The car you drive, house you live in or clothes you wear can be an occasion for heart lift, if you allow them to be. The external trappings say to the world, "I have made it," but internally, your neediness, weakness and insecurity is just as great as it has ever been.

For the person who suffers from heart lift, comparing himself with others who have less is necessary to the hydraulics of heart lift and feeling of superiority. It is not necessary to have a lot quantitatively in order to be guilty; you just need to have more or consider yourself better or superior to others. You could have two homeless men living in cardboard boxes, but if one has a newer, larger box, he may feel superior.

We all could possibly have been quite guilty of this. I once heard a message entitled, "Comparisonitis." The message dealt with the sin of comparing ourselves with people we feel superior to and the pride that result from these comparisons. Comparisonitis is a prelude to heart lift.

Earlier, we talked about Uzziah. We read that God made him to prosper because he sought God. The prosperity that Uzziah enjoyed was because of the position of his heart; it was a position of dependence and humility. The blessings accumulated as time passed and his heart inched ever upward. Upward mobility of this sort proved to be hazardous to Uzziah' health, wealth and general well-being.

The Bible says, in reference to Uzziah, "But when he was strong, his heart was lifted up to his destruction" 2 Chronicles 26:16. How many times do we cry out to God in our weakness yet have no need of Him when we feel strong?

We must be watchful of the heart being lifted up. God wants your hands to be lifted not your heart. He wants your hands high and your heart low. Heart lift is to man what locusts are to a vineyard. The flesh is always looking for a reason to lift the heart and place it on a pedestal where it does not belong.

You must not allow the blessings of God to change your heart toward Him. It is a change that is not immediately noticeable because of the subtlety with which it occurs. Heart lift occurs when you begin to take what God has done for granted or infringe on God's glory by attributing the blessings He has given to your own ability, intellect or savvy.

The blessings of God are not given in order to declare our superiority but to celebrate His glory. The flesh will use the blessings of God as an occasion for self-glorification and the feeling of "somebodiness" that you may have been striving for all your life.

We would not verbally acknowledge that but our actions say what our mouth does not. "What is it that you have that you did not receive? And if you received it, why do you glory as though you did not receive it." 1 Corinthians 4:7

You may be a very bright person, but who gave you the ability to quickly assimilate information and understand?

Who gave you the ability to verbalize your thoughts to the degree that everyone who hears you is spellbound?

Who gave you the business savvy to accumulate the financial wealth you have attained?

Who looked down on your neediness and turned junk into jewelry?

Who is the one that gave you the singing voice that is so sweet, it inspires everyone within the vicinity of its sound?

Who is it that takes the person who could not string two complete sentences together and make him a gifted orator whose gift has placed him before great men?

Who is the one that rescued you from the darkness of your past and gave you a future so bright the English vocabulary lacks adequate words to describe? It is God! It is God!

God gave all that you have, therefore, your heart must be humble and all boasting must be in Him.

9

When God Says No

"When God's answer is not what we desire, we must change our desire and embrace His answer."

2 Corinthians12:9-10 – "And he said unto me, My grace is sufficient for thee: for my strength is made perfect in weakness. Most gladly therefore will I rather glory in my infirmities, that the power of Christ may rest upon me.10Therefore I take pleasure in infirmities, in reproaches, in necessities, in persecutions, in distresses for Christ's sake: for when I am weak, then am I strong."

When our request falls outside of the sphere of what God desires for us, He has the right to say no and, at times, He does. There are times when you may come to understand why He said no. However, there will be times when you may never know or understand why. But, how can we reconcile God saying no with what Jesus said?

"For verily I say unto you, That whosoever shall say unto this mountain, Be thou removed, and be thou cast into the sea; and shall not doubt in his heart, but shall believe that those things which he saith shall come to pass; he shall have whatsoever he saith. Therefore, I say unto you, what thing so ever ye desire, when ye pray, believe that ye receive them, and ye shall have them" Mark 11:23-24.

"Whatsoever" either meant absolutely anything, which would also include things that are not good for you or it meant whatsoever within the context of what He desires us to have.

1 John 5:14-15 – "And this is the confidence that we have in him, that, if we ask anything according to his will, he heareth us.15And if we know that he hears us, whatsoever we ask, we know that we have the petitions that we desired of him."

In this scripture, we see that getting what you ask for has a context. The context is prayer offered in the will of God.

Jesus teaches us to pray when he said, "Thy will be done," not "Thy will be changed." C.H. Dodd wrote, "Prayer rightly considered is not a device for employing the resources of omnipotence to fulfill our own desire, but a means by which our desires may be redirected according to the mind of God, and made into channels for the forces of his will."

If this "whatsoever" means anything regardless of what it is, this would be tantamount to giving a child a loaded gun. You may believe that Christians would never ask God for anything that was not good for them. Many times, as James 4:3 states, "Ye ask and receive not because you ask amiss, that you may consume it upon you lust."

Amiss is akin to the Greek work kakos, which stands for "whatever is evil in character base." Kakos is antithetic to kalos, which is "fair, advisable and good in character" and to agathos, which is "beneficial, useful and good in act." Therefore, it denotes what is useless and bad. The use of kakos may be broadly divided as follows: of what is morally or ethically bad or of what is injurious and destructive.

I have asked for things I did not receive and so did Paul. 2 Corinthians12:7-8 says, "And lest I should be exalted above measure through the abundance of the revelations, there was given to me a thorn in flesh, the messenger of Satan to buffet me, lest I should be exalted above measure.8For this thing I besought the Lord thrice, that it might depart from me."

The thorn was a "whatsoever," but it was not removed. Paul did not receive what he asked for. Trusting God, even when He says no, is perhaps the greatest manifestation of our confidence in His love for us. God's purpose is more important than our convenience. As a matter of fact, his purpose is often the cause of our inconvenience, but it is also an occasion to experience the sufficiency of His grace.

2 Corinthians12:9-10 says, "And he said unto me, My grace is sufficient for thee: for my strength is made perfect in weakness. Most gladly therefore will I rather glory in my infirmities, that the power of Christ may rest upon me.10Therefore I take pleasure in infirmities, in reproaches, in necessities, in persecutions, in distresses for Christ's sake: for when I am weak, then am I strong."

Paul did not receive what he asked for, but he rejoiced in what he got.

"God's answers are wiser that our prayers." – Unknown

There is a great deal that I don't understand and I must trust God with those things. There was a member of the church who had been loyal supportive for over twenty years. She had a sixteen-year-old daughter whom she loved deeply. She took her daughter to the doctor's office because of a sore throat that she could not get rid of. After a barrage of tests, it was determined that the child had a very aggressive form of cancer and her condition began to deteriorate quickly. In spite of the news, the mother was undaunted in her faith. I was at the hospital when the doctor gave a very bad report. The mother looked at him with kind eyes, as though she was saying, "I hear what you are saying, but my daughter will be healed." In a matter of a few weeks, the child was dead. The mother and the entire church was devastated. She became very angry and bitter. She eventually stopped coming to church and stayed out of church for two years.

One day, she called and asked if she could meet with us and we agreed. We were so glad to see her and during the meeting, she asked us to forgive her for things she had said and done. She went on to tell us that after her daughter died, she spiraled downward. She said that every day, she would curse at God and say that He was not real. She said, "I would walk through the house and just use profanity towards God because He let my daughter die."

She said that even though she left God, He never left her and after two years, she began to reach out to Him with tears asking Him to forgive and restore her. God brought her back to Him and the church where she had served faithfully until she died. In bringing her back, God was gracious to us by answering our prayers for her restoration. My point is that sometimes we may not get what we hope for in this world, but we have a higher hope, a hope that is not restricted to this life. Paul said it best when he said, "If we only have hope in Christ in this life, we are, of all men, most miserable."

10

Prayer In Jesus' Name

"Prayer in Jesus name is more in the being of it that the saying of it."

Sometimes, we have faith in abundance, but we lack something central to prayer. What I am referring to is whether or not the prayer is in the name of Jesus. I believe that often, our prayers are more concerned with what we want as opposed to what He wants us to have. I don't believe that we can ever really pray in His name until we remove self from the center of our prayers. When God becomes the priority, our prayers are consistent with God being on the throne of our heart. It is not the verbal assertion that your prayer is in the name of Jesus that makes it so. I am not saying that you shouldn't declare your prayer, "In the name of Jesus." On the contrary, I believe that we should verbally declare in whose name we pray. However, I also believe that there is more to a prayer being in Jesus name that just saying it is.

Many times our prayers are fueled by so many things that have nothing to do with the name of Christ, yet we pray them in Jesus' name, expecting God to honor whatsoever we have asked.

We need help in prayer, as it is described in Romans 8:26, "Likewise the Spirit also helpeth our infirmities: for we know what we should pray for as we ought: but the Spirit itself maketh intercession for us with groaning which cannot be uttered."

Praying *in the name of Jesus* is not referring to an expression tacked on the end of a sentence that guarantees you will receive whatever you ask for. The phrase, "In the name of Jesus" has to do with authorization and the sphere within which God will grant us whatever we ask. For prayer to be in Jesus' name, it must agree with the character, provisions and the purpose of Jesus. There are many things that we ask for in His name that are not by virtue of their character. "In Jesus' name" denotes a sphere of identification and agreement.

When we come together, it must also be in His name. Matthew 18:20 states, "For where two or three are gathered together in my name, there I am in the midst of them." But even though persons may declare that they are gathered or they come in Jesus' name, the verbal assertion does not mandate truth. Jesus said, "For many shall come **in my name or using my name**, saying, I am Christ; and shall deceive many" Matthew 24:5. Jesus said that they would come in His name, but he did not say that their coming would actually be *in His name*. A person may say that he has gathered in Jesus' name or that he is praying in Jesus' name. But only when his coming, words and deeds are consistent with His name is it, in fact, *in His name*.

I heard a story about a fellow who owned a lumber company and hired a contractor to build a house. He said to the contractor, "When you go to my lumber company, whatever you ask, they will give it to you." The contractor went to the lumberyard to get supplies. When he got to the counter, he said, "I need a television. Joe said, 'Whatsoever I ask in his name, you would give it to me'." The person denied the request. The contractor asked, "Why didn't you give me the television?" The fellow behind the counter said, "Because a television does not identify with the purpose of Joe, which is to build a house. You are to build the house, not furnish it."

Lumber is within the context of Joe's purpose and nails are within the context of Joe's purpose. However, a television is not consistent with Joe's purpose and he only authorized those things that were consistent with his purpose. Joe meant whatsoever, but he meant it within the context of why the contractor was hired.

You cannot separate the name of the person from the purpose of the person. So it is with Jesus; you cannot separate His name from His character, provisions or purpose and expect God to honor what has been asked. This is why prayer must not be rooted in selfishness because it has to do with the purpose of someone else.

Jesus came to do the will of the Father and His prayers were consistent with promoting the Father's purpose. Jesus said, in John 14:13, "Whatsoever ye ask **in My name**, that I will do that the Father may be glorified in the Son." Verbally saying *in the name of Jesus* no more guarantees that you will receive whatsoever you ask for any more than a water baptism guarantees that you are a part of the body of Christ.

When you are baptized in water, it is to symbolize visibly what has **already** been accomplished spiritually. The act of water baptism is to agree with a spiritual reality that has occurred in a person's life. Therefore, when one is baptized, it is only legitimate when there is agreement between the act of water baptism and a person being immersed into the body of Christ by trusting in the finished work of Christ. A person may be baptized using whatever formula they choose and the baptism might not be legitimate if that person has not trusted in Jesus as Savior. When our prayers agree with the interest, character, provision and purpose of Jesus, only then can we pray in His name.

11

Prayer and Praying Men

As I studied and read many articles on prayer and praying men, I was blessed by their insights and I wanted to share some of them with you. I could not include them all, though I wish I could have. As you read what they said and lived concerning prayer, I hope that you are as equally blessed as I was.

Samuel Chadwick – Path of Prayer

If only the Church of Christ could be impelled to prayer, today's crisis would be met. If only the people of God could be baptized into a passion of prayer, spiritual life and power would quicken, miracles would return and multitudes would be added unto the Lord!

Why do we not set ourselves to prayer? The remedy is sure and simple and the need is urgent and acknowledged. Why is it so slow in getting to work? What could be simpler than that? And yet the Scriptures speak of it as toil and labor.

Prayer taxes all the resources of mind and heart. Jesus Christ wrought many mighty works without any sign of effort. There was in His marvelous works the ease of omnipotence, but of His prayers, it is said, He "offered up prayers and supplications with strong crying and tears" (Heb. 5:7). There was no strain in healing diseases, raising the dead and stilling the tempest, but in prayer, there was agony and the sweat of blood.

Prayer is conflict and all who have shared His intercession have found it a travail of anguish. Great saints have always been mighty in prayer and their triumphs have always been the outcome of pain. They wrestled in agony with breaking hearts and weeping eyes until they were assured they had prevailed. They spent cold winter nights in prayer. They lay on the ground weeping, pleading and came out of the conflict physically spent, but spiritually victorious. They wrestled with principalities and powers, contended with the world rulers of Satan's kingdom, and grappled with spiritual foes in the heavenly sphere. A lost art!

Today, in the fellowship of believers, there is little power in prayer. There is a marked absence of travail. There is much phrasing, but little pleading. Prayer is no longer a passion! The powerlessness of the Church has no other explanation. The counselors of the Church need seek no other cause. To be prayerless is to be both passionless and powerless.

"The secret of Elijah's power in prayer was that he 'prayed in his prayer.'" That is the translation given in the margin of the Authorized Version. He "prayed earnestly" is given in the text, and "fervently" in the Revised Version, with the note in the margin that says the Greek definition is literally, "with prayer." He prayed with prayer; he prayed in his prayer. That is to say, he really prayed his prayers. His whole personality was in his supplication. He really wanted what he asked and he did so fervently, really meaning what he said.

Can that kind of prayer be taught? It is the prayer that prevails. Formal routine of temple-service and the regular reading of words of second-hand inspiration and no understanding are neither acceptable to God, nor profitable to man. They are vain repetitions. There is much praying that avails nothing, so far as we can judge. Prayers are measured neither by time, nor by number, but by intensity. There are prayers that are impassioned, but get no answer and there are things for which we know we ought to pray for in an agony of prayer, but there is no power to pray. We do not know how to pray.

There is no way to learn to pray but by praying. No reasoned philosophy of prayer ever taught a soul to pray. There have been souls that were mighty in prayer and they learned to pray. There was a period in their lives when they were as others in the matter of prayer, but they became mighty with God and prevailed. In every instance, there was a crisis of grace, but it was in the discipline of grace that they discovered the secret of power. They were known as men of God because they were men of prayer. Some of them were renamed, such as Jacob and Simon and Saul. They were called "Praying John", "Praying Mary", "Praying Bramwell" and "Praying Hyde". Our Methodist fathers were mighty in prayer. They saved England by prayer. They shook the gates of hell by prayer. They opened the windows of heaven by prayer. How did they learn to pray? They learned to pray by being much in prayer. They did not talk about prayer; they prayed. They did not argue about prayer; they prayed.

GEORGE MUELLER – Man of Prayer

George Mueller was born less than a decade before Charles Dickens in 1805, so he was certainly aware of all the horrors of society that the famed novelist describes in his works: workhouses, prisons, filth and disease, lack of concern for the poor and homeless – all the things about which Ebenezer Scrooge in his unredeemed state could care less for. But Mueller did care, deeply, and in 1834, he decided to do something about it. He and his best friend, Henry Craik, founded the Scriptural Knowledge Institution (SKI) in Bristol, England, with one of their prime objectives being to establish Orphan Homes for the many homeless children in Great Britain.

But Mueller and Craik had no money, nor did they intend to ask anyone for it. They believed that God would provide everything they needed without patronage, without requests for contributions and without debts. All they had to do was pray and God would provide. For 64 years, that was how George Mueller operated. In that course of time, he built The Orphanage campus at Ashley Down, where he cared for and educated over 18,000 children, educated over 100,000 more in other schools at the Orphanage's expense, distributed hundreds of thousands of Bibles and tens of millions of religious tracts, supported about 150 missionaries, travelled over 200,000 miles as a missionary himself and shared the Gospel with over 3 million people around the world. And in all that time, he never asked for one penny from anyone, his children never missed a meal and he never had a debt. That is the remarkable record of George Mueller.

Here are some of the ways he prayed:

First, he never shared a need with anyone but God. Second, when he had a need, he opened his Bible, searched for a promise that fit that need and then meditated on that scripture. Mueller believed in the power of thinking through scripture as much as he believed in the power of prayer. Third, he pleaded for that promise before God. And he didn't just pray for money; he prayed for individuals, as well. Sometimes, Mueller prayed for someone for as long as fifty years. He didn't stop praying for anyone or anything until he got his request. That's how convinced he was that God would answer his prayers. Through his prayers, Mueller obtained the modern-day equivalent of $150 million for his charities, he led tens, if not, hundreds of thousands to the Lord and he lived to be 93 years old. That was the power of his faith and life.

D.L. Moody
By Gregg Quiggle, dean, International Study Programs

In 1923, one of Dwight Lyman Moody's closest associates, R. A. Torrey, preached a sermon titled, "Why God Used D. L. Moody." In the sermon, Torrey gave seven reasons why God used Mr. Moody. One of the seven Torrey identified was that, "Mr. Moody was in the deepest and most meaningful sense a man of prayer." Even a cursory glance at Moody's life confirms Torrey's evaluation.

Early in his life as a believer, Moody came to learn of the importance and benefit of prayer. He had begun his life of faith as a result of the work of a Sunday school teacher in 1855 and shortly thereafter, he struck out for Chicago. There, he became involved in a prayer based revival that swept through the major cities in America. He immersed himself in the meetings, rarely missing an evening of prayer and they became foundational for how he later approached ministry. In fact, virtually everywhere he traveled over the course of his life, he organized prayer meetings.

During these years, Moody befriended the godly owner of his boarding house. Mrs. H. Phillips, or "Mother" Phillips as she was commonly known, was a stalwart at the First Baptist Church and she schooled Moody on the necessity of faithful prayer. He took those lessons to heart as prayer became a central part of his life.

Moody always demanded intense and focused prayer in preparation for his revival campaigns. When he began new projects he often called on the students and faculty of his schools to devote themselves to fasting and prayer.

Emphasizing the importance and power of prayer was so important to Moody it was one of the predominant characteristics of the schools in both Northfield and Chicago. His student conferences in Northfield featured 6:00 a.m. prayer meetings and he organized prayer meetings for children. Later, he would say, "Some of the happiest nights I ever had were in these children's prayer meetings."

D.L. Moody not only worked hard for the Lord, but he also he prayed hard as he worked. His life and enduring work stand as an eloquent testimony to fruits of fervent prayer.

James 5:16: "The prayer of a righteous person has great effectiveness."

Leonard Ravenhill

There's nothing more transfiguring than prayer. People often ask, "Why do you insist on prayer so much?" The answer is very simple. Because Jesus did. You could change the title of the Gospel according to St. Luke to the Gospel of Prayer. It's the prayer life of Jesus. The other evangelists say that Jesus was in the Jordan and the Spirit descended on Him as a dove – Luke says it was *while He was praying* that the Spirit descended on Him. The other evangelists say that Jesus chose 12 disciples – Luke says it was after He spent *a night in prayer* that He chose 12 disciples. The other evangelists say that Jesus died on a cross – Luke says that even when He was dying, *Jesus was praying* for those who persecuted Him. The other evangelists say Jesus went on a mount and He was transfigured – Luke says it was *while He was praying* that He was transfigured.

There's nothing more transfiguring than prayer. The Scriptures say that the disciples went to bed, but Jesus went *to pray,* as was His custom. It was His custom to pray. Now, Jesus was the Son of God and he was definitely anointed for His ministry. If Jesus needed all that time in prayer, don't you and I need time in prayer? If Jesus needed it in every crisis, don't you and I need it in every crisis?

12

Christian Prayer Quotes

"If I fail to spend two hours in prayer each morning, the devil gets the victory through the day. I have so much business I cannot get on without spending three hours daily in prayer." – Martin Luther

"Men may spurn our appeals, reject our message, oppose our arguments, despise our persons, but they are helpless against our prayers." – Sidlow Baxter

"Satan does not care how many people read about prayer if only he can keep them from praying." – Paul E. Billheimer

"Don't pray when you feel like it. Have an appointment with the Lord and keep it. A man is powerful on his knees." – Corrie ten Boom

"Talking to men for God is a great thing, but talking to God for men is greater still." – E.M. Bounds

"The men who have done the most for God in this world have been early on their knees. He who fritters away the early morning, its opportunity and freshness, in other pursuits than seeking God will make poor headway seeking Him the rest of the day. If God is not first in our thoughts and efforts in the morning, He will be in the last place the remainder of the day." – E.M. Bounds

"The little estimate we put on prayer is evidence from the little time we give to it." – E.M. Bounds

"It is necessary to iterate and reiterate that prayer, as a mere habit, as a performance gone through by routine or in a professional way, is a dead and rotten thing." – E.M. Bounds

"Satan trembles when he sees the weakest Christian on his knees." – William Cowper

"If the church wants a better pastor, it only needs to pray for the one it has."

"Prayer will make a man cease from sin, or sin will entice a man to cease from prayer." – John Bunyon

"He who has learned to pray has learned the greatest secret of a holy and happy life." – William Law

"Prayer is not overcoming God's reluctance, but laying hold of His willingness." – Martin Luther

"The one concern of the devil is to keep Christians from praying. He fears nothing from prayerless studies, prayerless work and prayerless religion. He laughs at our toil, mocks at our wisdom, but he trembles when we pray." – Samuel Chadwick

"I would rather teach one man to pray than ten men to preach." – Charles Spurgeon

"The man who mobilizes the Christian church to pray will make the greatest contribution to world evangelization in history." – Andrew Murray

"If I could hear Christ praying for me in the next room, I would not fear a million enemies. Yet distance makes no difference. He is praying for me." – Robert Murray McCheyne

Spurgeon's "boiler room". Five young college students were spending a Sunday in London, so they went to hear the famed C.H. Spurgeon preach. While waiting for the doors to open, the students were greeted by a man who asked, "Gentlemen, let me show you around. Would you like to see the heating plant of this church?" They were not particularly interested, for it was a hot day in July. But they didn't want to offend the stranger, so they consented. The young men were taken down a stairway, a door was quietly opened and their guide whispered, "This is our heating plant." Surprised, the students saw 700 people bowed in prayer, seeking a blessing on the service that was soon to begin in the auditorium above. Softly closing the door, the gentleman then introduced himself. It was none other than Charles Spurgeon.

"Prayer is the greatest of all forces, because it honors God and brings him into active aid." – E.M. Bounds

"Prayer is often not easy work this is why my soul sometimes shrinks from prayer."– Michael Canion

"Prayer should not be regarded "as a duty which must be performed, but rather as a privilege to be enjoyed, a rare delight that is always revealing some new beauty." – E.M. Bounds

"The battle of prayer is against two things in the earthlies: wandering thoughts, and lack of intimacy with God's character as revealed in His word. Neither can be cured at once, but they can be cured by discipline." – Oswald Chambers

"Four things let us ever keep in mind: God hears prayer, God heeds prayer, God answers prayer, and God delivers by prayer." – E. M. Bounds

"...True prayer is measured by weight, not by length. A single groan before God may have more fullness of prayer in it than a fine oration of great length." – C. H. Spurgeon

"The word of God is the food by which prayer is nourished and made strong." – E. M. Bounds

"The closer we get to God, the closer we realize we need to come. We therefore live constantly coming, each step we take is one less step we have to make . Lord grant us the grace to keep coming." – Michael Canion

"Therefore, whether the desire for prayer is on you or not, get to your closet at the set time. Shut yourself in with God, wait upon Him, seek His face, realize Him, pray." – R. F. Horton

"Time spent alone with God is not wasted. It changes us, it changes our surroundings and every Christian who would live the life that counts, and who would have power for service must take time to pray." – M.E. Andross

"Make time to pray. The great freight and passenger trains are never too busy to stop for fuel. No matter how congested the yards may be, no matter how crowded the schedules are, no matter how many things demand the attention of the trainmen, those trains always stop for fuel." – M.E. Andross

"If the Christian does not allow prayer to drive sin out of his life, sin will drive prayer out of his life. Like light and darkness, the two cannot dwell together." – M.E. Andross

"We must begin to believe that God, in the mystery of prayer, has entrusted us with a force that can move the Heavenly world, and can bring its power down to earth." – Andrew Murray

"Prayer is a spiritual law which cooperates with the mind of God. It has more in it than merely petition. It clothes itself in reality and power, with the force of God Himself. It is an attitude of spirit and mind. Language is secondary in true prayer." – Gossner

"What the church needs today is not more machinery or better, not new organizations or more novel methods, but men whom the Holy Ghost can use— men of prayer, men mighty in prayer." – E.M. Bounds

"Prayer does not fit us for the greater work; prayer is the greater work." – Oswald Chambers

"It is not enough to begin to pray, nor to pray aright, nor is it enough to continue for a time to pray, but we must patiently, believingly, continue in prayer until we obtain an answer." – George Müller

"Those persons who know the deep peace of God, the unfathomable peace that passeth all understanding, are always men and women of much prayer." – R. A. Torrey

"The trouble with nearly everybody who prays is that he says 'Amen' and runs away before God has a chance to reply. Listening to God is far more important than giving Him our ideas." – Frank Laubach

"Prayer is not learned in a classroom but in the closet." – E. M. Bounds

"Prayer is weakness leaning on omnipotence." – W. S. Bowd

"The main lesson about prayer is just this: Do it! Do it! Do it! You want to be taught to pray. My answer is pray and never faint, and then you shall never fail..." – John Laidlaw

"A man who is intimate with God will never be intimidated by men." – Leonard Ravenhill

"Prayer is buried, and lost and Heaven weeps. If all prayed, the wicked would flee from our midst or to the refuge." – Evan Roberts

"Out of a very intimate acquaintance with D. L. Moody, I wish to testify that he was a far greater prayer than he was preacher. Time and time again, he was confronted by obstacles that seemed insurmountable, but he always knew the way to overcome all difficulties. He knew the way to bring to pass anything that needed to be brought to pass. He knew and believed in the

deepest depths of his soul that nothing was too hard for the Lord, and that prayer could do anything that God could do." – R. A. Torrey (Emphasis added)

"It is in the field of prayer that life's critical battles are lost or won. We must conquer all our circumstances there. We must first of all bring them there. We must survey them there. We must master them there. In prayer we bring our spiritual enemies into the Presence of God and we fight them there. Have you tried that? Or have you been satisfied to meet and fight your foes in the open spaces of the world?" – J. H. Jowett

"There has never been a spiritual awakening in any country or locality that did not begin in united prayer." – A.T. Pierson

"The greatest thing anyone can do for God or man is pray." – S.D. Gordon

"I will never truly seek God until I realize how destitute I am without Him." – Michael Canion

"If I fail to spend two hours in prayer each morning, the devil gets the victory through the day. I have so much business, I cannot get on without spending three hours daily in prayer." – Martin Luther

"Men may spurn our appeals, reject our message, oppose our arguments, despise our persons, but they are helpless against our prayers." – Sidlow Baxter

"The men who have done the most for God in this world have been early on their knees. He who fritters away the early morning, its opportunity and freshness, in other pursuits than seeking God will make poor headway seeking Him the rest of the day. If God is not first in our thoughts and efforts in the morning, He will be in the last place the remainder of the day." – E.M. Bounds

"The little estimate we put on prayer is evidence from the little time we give to it." – E.M. Bounds

"He who has learned to pray has learned the greatest secret of a holy and happy life." – William Law

"I would rather teach one man to pray than ten men to preach." – Charles Spurgeon

"The man who mobilizes the Christian church to pray will make the greatest contribution to world evangelization in history." – Andrew Murray

"If I could hear Christ praying for me in the next room, I would not fear a million enemies. Yet distance makes no difference. He is praying for me." – Robert Murray McCheyne

On persevering prayer: "I look at a stone cutter hammering away at a rock a hundred times without so much as a crack showing in it. Yet at the 101st blow it splits in two. I know it was not the one blow that did it, but all that had gone before."

"Intimacy is the place of power. Time is the price of intimacy, boldness and power are its reward." – Michael Canion

"In the pursuit of intimacy, there is no substitute for unhurried time spent with God." – Michael Canion

"The word of God is the food by which prayer is nourished and made strong." – E. M. Bounds

"Hurry is the enemy of intimacy." – Michael Canion

"What the church needs today is not more machinery or better, not new organizations or more novel methods, but men whom the Holy Ghost can use— men of prayer, men mighty in prayer." – E.M. Bounds

"Prayer can never be in excess." – C. H. Spurgeon

"Ministers who do not spend two hours a day in prayer are not worth a dime a dozen, degrees or no degrees." – Leonard Ravenhill

"He who runs from God in the morning will scarcely find Him the rest of the day." – John Bunyan

"Each time, before you intercede, be quiet first, and worship God in His glory. Think of what He can do, and how He delights to hear the prayers of His redeemed people. Think of your place and privilege in Christ and expect great things!" – Andrew Murray

"Intercession is truly universal work for the Christian. No place is closed to intercessory prayer. No continent , no nation, no organization, no city, no office. There is no power on earth that can keep intercession out." – Richard Halverson

"No one is a firmer believer in the power of prayer than the devil; not that he practices it, but he suffers from it." – Guy H. King (Try practicing this concept)

"Prayer does not fit us for the greater work; prayer is the greater work." – Oswald Chanbers

Three is nothing wrong with us that a closer walk with God won't cure." – Michael Canion

When it comes to waiting on God it is not a matter of how long you wait but how well you wait. Lord help us to wait well." – Michael Canion

The thing that God desires most is the thing that most are unwilling to give: unhurried time with Him." – Michael Canion